Dropshipping:

Road to $10,000 per month of Passive Income Doesn't Have to be Difficult! Learn more about Social Media Advertising, Facebook Advertising, Shopify Ecommerce and Ebay

tertiary copy of the work or a recorded copy and is only allowed with express written consent from the Publisher. All additional rights reserved.

The information in the following pages is broadly considered to be a truthful and accurate account of facts and as such any inattention, use or misuse of the information in question by the reader will render any resulting actions solely under their purview. There are no scenarios in which the publisher or the original author of this work can be in any fashion deemed liable for any hardship or damages that may befall them after undertaking information described herein.

Additionally, the information in the following pages is intended only for informational purposes and should thus be thought of as universal. As befitting its nature, it is presented without assurance regarding its prolonged validity or interim quality. Trademarks that are mentioned are done without written consent and can in no way be considered an endorsement from the trademark holder.

Table of Contents

Introduction

Every day, the thought of running your own online business becomes more and more vivid and pronounced. Every day, you work on getting this dream a reality whether it is reading about doing your own business, saving up money, talking to people, and finding your niche - you are making small progress, and then one day, you just do it. You open your laptop, you sign up for a platform, and you're establishing the foundations of your dream.

The reality is, with the internet and using the dropship business model, setting up and running your own online business is easier compared to setting up a brick-and-stone store. With a few simple clicks, you are already on your way in setting up an e-commerce site and actively investing in your success.

What is Dropshipping?

Dropshipping is an element of retail fulfillment practice in the standard retail model that allows a store selling products and merchandise to not hold its own inventory or, in other words, do away with keeping their products in stock, or shipping their products to their customers on their own or owning a warehouse to store its products.

In this case, whenever there is an order for the product, the seller purchases the item from a third-party vendor and this third-party vendor ships it directly to the customer. The retailer partner with a dropship supplier does the manufacturing, warehousing, packaging, and shipping of these products on the retailer's behalf. The merchant does not see or handles the said product.

Chapter 1 - Pros & Cons of Dropshipping

Dropshipping is different from the other retails models due to this major factor - the retail owner or merchant does not own inventory or stock. The merchant, instead, purchases this inventory as and when it is needed from their third-party supplier that focuses on manufacturing or wholesaling in order to meet customer demands.

In other words, drop shipping works as below:

- The customer makes an order for a product seen on the merchant's online store.
- The merchant records the order purchase and automatically sends this to the dropship supplier, complete with order details and customer information.
- The dropship supplier packages the product and ships it according to the customer's given information.

This is an extremely effective and attractive business model as it eliminates the purpose of the merchant to have a physical business venue like an office space or even a warehouse. All they ever need is internet access, a website, and a device connected to the internet to upload, update, and store information on their products and services if any.

Pros of Dropshipping

There are plenty of benefits to this dropshipping business model. These are:

- It is extremely easy to set up. Unlike setting up a brick-and-mortar business space, this retail model only involves just three steps which are:

  i) finding the supplier

  ii) setting up a good website and once that is done

  iii) selling your products and services

- This model is easy to understand and implement especially for those new to the e-commerce industry

- To set up your business with the dropship model, the cost involved is literally next to nothing. Unlike in traditional business models where the major costs go into the setting and running of the operations, in dropshipping, this step is eliminated and all the cost you need to think of is the applications you need to run your website, domain registration, hosting as well as themes you use.

- There are no unreasonably high overhead costs involved. The merchant or business owner can do away with renting or buying warehouses to store their products and also do away with utility bills that come with it. The costs of managing the website are all they need to worry about.

- Dropshipping risks are significantly lower because there is little to no pressure about selling inventory.

- This type of business model can be run from anywhere, meaning the business owner or merchant is location-independent. There is no warehouse, no sales location, no offices, not much employees, and no hassles.

- There is little to absolutely no commitment to a physical space requirement which means the business owner can run their business by the beach, in their home, or while flying on the plane. All you ever need is an internet connection and your laptop or iPad or Tablet or any device you can access the internet with.

- You can sell just about anything over the internet and there's a dropship supplier for almost anything out there. Either sell only one product or a mix of products - it is entirely up to you. Just find your niche and the right dropship supplier you need.

- You will have more time and resources to look into scaling your business. With traditional business models, the more you profit, the more work you have to put in and the more you need to invest in the resource section. Of course, even with the dropshipping model, you need to put in some investment but not a huge amount. Dropshipping enables you to send more orders to your supplier. From here on, you let them handle everything else while all you need to do is earn profits.

- Dropship also reduces losses on damaged goods. Shipment is directly from supplier to customer and because there is lesser shipment steps involved, the risk of the items being damaged is also reduced.

Cons of Dropshipping

Where there are pros, there are also cons even when it comes to dropshipping. Here are some of them:

- You will receive slightly lower profit margins compared to sourcing from a manufacturer or a wholesaler. Dropship suppliers will charge you higher prices depending on your niche, requirements, and location and this will cut into your profit margins.
- You have to bear complete liability if anything goes wrong, even if it is the supplier's fault. The customer purchases the product from your site- the merchant's website. In the

event, something happens or if the supplier doesn't keep their end of the bargain or messes up, it is still the merchant's fault. Your customers will contact you because you are the face of the brand. This is why it is extremely important to hire the right dropship supplier.

- You have lower control over the creative process. Your customers will have lesser satisfaction with your product because you will not be able to determine personalized packaging or the branding of the shipped products- this is dependent on the supplier.

- You have less control over how your product is presented during the fulfillment and delivery process as this is the supplier's job to ship the products to the customers. However, having the right supplier and establishing a good relationship with them will give you better control as some suppliers will go the extra mile in ensuring your creative process is delivered through the product. However, this may cost more.

- There may be more issues, especially when it comes to shipping. Selling multiple products is a good idea as it can increase sales and your profit. However, it can also pose a problem if the merchant has too many suppliers to deal with for each product they sell. Also, different suppliers will change different shipping costs as this would depend on where they are located and what kind of product you have.

- The competition in dropshipping retail is extremely high due to the attractiveness and the popularity of this business model. Unless the merchant caters to an extremely specific niche, the competition is detrimental.

- It is hard to keep track of the inventory from the supplier because of miscommunications due to cancellations and having backorders. However, with new software coming in and improved communication abilities, this matter can be solved. Of course, this software also comes with a price and may also increase your overhead costs.

How Viable and Profitable is Dropshipping?

Profit margins for dropshipping usually range from 15% to 45%. For consumer goods such as luxury items and durables, the profit margin can be up to 100%. When it comes to dropshipping, it entirely depends on the kind of niche you are in and then getting the right supplier. You do not want to enter a heavily saturated market.

One of the better ways to ensure higher margins is to source directly from the manufacturer and not the vendor/supplier. This cuts out the middleman. Once the business gains traction, it can become an effective money-making means that only involves little input. The potential to earn up to one million dollars is real, although not for every dropshipping business.

Who is Dropshipping For?

If you are a first-timer entering the online business, then dropshipping is a great business model, to begin with. It is low-risk and low-investment which is great for novices starting their own business. It does not involve much monetary gamble.

It is ideal for someone who is the current owner of a retail store and already has an inventory but looking to reach newer, wider markets. This business model, however, does not give you amazing results from the get-go. Dropshipping margins are relatively lower so this might not bode well for a startup brand because these businesses do not have ultimate control where customer satisfaction, related to brand experience, and branding is concerned.

Here are the types of entrepreneurs where drop shipping will benefit:

- The Validating Entrepreneur

Dropshipping is a great way to test new products or even new startup products before an entrepreneur can begin heavily ingesting into the inventory required to sell. This makes it the perfect business model for entrepreneurs that require high levels of product validation before they begin investing heavily.

- The Budget Entrepreneur

Dropship qualifies as the least expensive business model for online selling because you do not need to purchase inventory upfront. Due to this, the dropshipping method sells effectively for entrepreneurs that are on a budget or are looking to keep startup costs low.

- The First Time Entrepreneur

Selling online is not as easy as it seems to be, so for the first time online entrepreneur, the dropshipping method works well. Understanding how to market the product online and drive and convert traffic takes time to figure out as well as optimize. Dropshipping allows online entrepreneurs to learn the ropes of online commerce, conversion, and driving traffic before they begin investing thousands in an inventory.

- The Multi-Variety Entrepreneur

Dropshipping is an ideal model to use for retailers who want to sell a variety of products simple for the reason that you do not need to purchase inventory upfront.

Who Isn't Drop Shipping For?

- The Brand centric entrepreneur

Building a brand around a product is difficult but the rewards are long-term and worthwhile. However, it is exponentially difficult to build a brand using the dropshipping retail method because there are plenty of other elements connected to the entire customer experience that the brand-centric entrepreneur will not be part of. For instance, there will be times that when a customer has made a purchase for a product, you as the merchant find it's sold out with the dropship supplier. This is not only inconvenient for you as the merchant but also frustrating to the customer. It is even more frustrating to coordinate between dropshipper and customer to determine a solution. Since you are not shipping the product on your own, you also do not have control of the packaging which is an extension of the brand experience.

While some merchants are okay with that, asking yourself if this bothers you will help determine if dropshipping is for you. You also will not be able to create a relationship with shipping companies because you do not do the shipping. When something goes wrong in the shipping process, coordinating with the shipping companies can prove to be difficult. You need to coordinate with the shipping account representative, who is already busy and this might take a few days to sort out.

- The Margin Focused Entrepreneur

One of the biggest problems with dropshipping is its thin margin lines. Gross margins for traditional dropshipping products are around 10 to 20%. After you pay off your credit card transaction fees, e-commerce fees, and other online services, you are looking at only a small percent of your margin left. While there are online entrepreneurs who earn big, up to a million dollars of revenue each year, their profit margins are around 40k to 50k once all these fees are deducted.

- The Non-Creative Marketer

With more manufacturers, chances are that they are also dropshippers of their own products and they also have the same exact goals in sales which are about 30% coming from direct-to-consumer sales and this is usually from their own e-commerce site. This would mean that to sell their product, you are competing directly with your own supplier. This supplier has many other advantages such as higher margins than you on the same existing product. Competing with them head-to-head is a waste of time and resource because most of the time, they win out all because they can afford to. You need to be creative and exploit other channels that they are not using in order to acquire the same target market and beat them. Relying on Google Adwords or Facebook Ads isn't going to cut it.

Chapter 2 - Running your Dropshipping Business

Running Your Dropshipping Business

In this chapter, you should or must already have the fundamentals of dropshipping down pat at least enough to contemplate launching a business in dropshipping.

But hang on, before you start, you will want to look into some really important business and financial steps if you are truly serious in getting your new venture out in the open and the very fact that you are reading this book says that you are SERIOUS about dropshipping.

Some of these procedures are a must-do while others are just good to do. However, identifying them and dealing with it now will save you time and challenges that may come ahead.

The Commitment Required

Like with any business, building a successful business in dropshipping will require your commitment and long-term perspective. However, do not set yourself up for disappointment too fast, too soon. While you can make profits in your business, but even before you get there, you need to approach your business with a more realistic mindset and set practical expectations with regards to investment and profitability. When it comes to dropshipping, your major investments are time or money.

Investing Time

Investing your time is a much favored approached compared to investing money from the get-go. This method is ideal for these reasons:

- Investing your time will enable you to learn how dropshipping operates inside and out. Reading books can only get you so far- it helps you start out but it is crucial to learn the ropes on your own so you can see your business grow and scale.

- Investing your time will help you understand and know your target customers as well as your market, which will help you make informed decisions as your business grows.

- Investing your time also means you are less likely to spend large sums of money on 'nice-to-have' projects that are not a must-have for your business success.

- Investing your time also enables you to develop new skills that will make you a better entrepreneur as your business grows.

While you do want to quit that 9 to 5 job and spend all your time on building your dropshipping business, realistically, you and most people cannot afford to do it, unless you have an investor ready to help you out or you have enough savings to help you stay afloat for at least a minimum of 6 months. That said, it is not impossible either. You need to put some challenging time ahead but it is possible to continue dropshipping even while on a 9 to 5 as long as you set appropriate expectations for your business. As you grow, you can slowly transition into working full time on your business as your profitability and cash flow will eventually allow this, plus, you need to focus more time on your retails business and this might interfere in your daily job.

If you do get a chance to work on your business full-time, best to take it. It is the best choice to increase your chances of success as well as increase your profit potential. Whatever time you have, focus your attention on marketing, especially in the early days when you want to build momentum. Focusing full time on your dropshipping business and a strong focus on marketing and promoting your business will help you get that average full-time income of $50,000.

In doing this, there are two things to keep in mind:

- When your dropshipping business gets up and running, the hard part comes in maintaining your site, but this may take less time than earning that amount of money than from a 9 to 5 job. Your biggest investment would pay off in terms of scalability and efficiency that the dropshipping model offers.

- You will be creating more than just an income stream as and when you are building your business. You are also building yourself an asset which could be sold off in the future. You also want to consider the equity value of the business that you are accruing as well as the cash flow that is generated when looking at your true returns.

Investing Money

You have the ability to create and establish a dropshipping business by investing a whole lot of money but this is not the best advice. The most success you will achieve is when you have done the dirty work with your business. It is extremely crucial to be the person who is deeply invested in the success of your business building it from the ground up. Or at least have someone who is that person. It is extremely crucial for you and your business partner to understand how your business works in each level.

While investing a lot of money in your dropshipping business is not something recommended, because actually, you still need to have some amount of cash somewhere in the range of $1,000 for launching and operational costs for hosting fees.

Deciding on a Business Structure

Part of taking your business seriously is to set up a legitimate business entity. Here are some of the most common business structures that you can look into for e-commerce:

- **Sole Proprietorship**

  This is a simple and straightforward business structure that one can implement in your dropshipping business. However, it also means that it offers you no protection from personal liability which means if in the event your business is sued, your personal assets are also part of this equation. On the other hand, requirements for filing are minimal and all you have to do is make sure you report on both your personal taxes as well as the earnings from your business.

- **Limited Liability Company (LLC)**

  With an LLC, your personal assets are protected because you can establish your business as a separate legal entity. This type of business structure does offer more protection than a sole proprietorship, although it is not foolproof. In this kind of business structure, you will need to adhere to certain filing requirements as well as pay certain fees.

- **C Corporation**

  C corporations, when set up properly, offer the most liability protection. Most businesses set up as C Corporation. This business structure is more on the expensive side and it is also subjected to double taxation as the income does not pass to the shareholders directly.

So which of these structures would you choose?

Most business owners will go for LLC or sole proprietorship. For dropshipping, it is recommended

28

to go with an LLC because it offers a better trade-off regarding autonomy from personal finances and costs and liability protection.

Making sure your finances are in order

When you start out a business, do not make the mistake of blending your business finances with your personal finances. This is confusing and audit nightmare on both a personal and professional level not to mention that it will make accounting difficult as well. Keeping your business and personal finances separate is one of the best advice you can use no matter what kind of business you are in, dropshipping or brick-and-mortar. Opening new accounts under your business's registered name is a great way to start.

Here are the bank accounts you need to open:

- **Business Checking Account**

All of your business finances need to be run through using one main checking account. Any and all of your business revenue must be deposited into this account and any expense for your business must be withdrawn from it. This would make things easier for you, the business owner as well for your accountant.

- **PayPal Account**

PayPal accounts are great to have on your e-commerce site, especially if you plan to accept payments via PayPal. For this, you will also want a business account tied to your e-commerce website.

- **Credit Card**

As credit cards are preferred payments by suppliers, credit cards are preferred methods of payment by your customers, too. In that same mindset, you should also have a business credit card for the business expenses as well as for your inventory purchases for dropshipping. There will be plenty of purchases that you will make from your suppliers and using a credit card connected to your business account enables you to gain some serious rewards. Look around for cards that give you rewards for things like travel, online transactions, and certain types of merchandise that you will most likely be purchasing more often.

Collecting Sales Tax

Of course, taxes are something that you must know. You will need to collect sales tax if you fall into this category:

- The state your business is operating from collects sales tax
- An order is made by a person living in your state

In orders made by people residing in other states and even in states that have your own sales tax, you do not need to collect a tax. These tax laws for online merchants are beneficial, especially if you are new to dropshipping and your business is still considered small.

Local Business Licenses

Businesses need business licenses and these licenses need to be renewed on a regular basis. For dropshipping businesses, the requirements may differ and these will likely involved operations from home offices. When starting your dropshipping business, look into what your local laws and regulations require, if anything.

STEP 1: Finding your Niche in Dropshipping

It may sound overwhelming to find your niche in business because there are plenty of things that you can get involved in. While it does sound overwhelming, it is not hard as there are a few methods that you can employ to find that perfect niche that would give you profits. Here are some methods that you may want to try in looking for the right niche:

Tip #1- Brainstorming

Brainstorming is always effective for practically anything you need to work on - ideas, solutions, methods and finding the right niche. To begin brainstorming ideas for your niches, meet up with your business partner or like-minded friends who will be able to help you or someone you trust. Friends and family who know you and your business partner are the most ideal. Next, you want to block off time to focus on your brainstorming, so set a meeting, time, and date for this.

When you meet, one of the things to think about is the items that you or your business partner or friends have bought online or recently purchased. Write these things down, even if it perplexes you. There will be many profitable niches out there that you can try but that does not mean you should rush into the business of dropshipping. When you have your niches, list them down and filter them according to:

- Competition: Look out for other dropshipping stores and look into the kinds of products that are oversaturated. You do not want to get into selling these.

- Returns: Do not go for products that have different sizes and style preferences - they usually come with high return rates.

- Loyalty: Avoid getting into niches that are dominated by a national brand.

- Weight: A high-priced product will be the winning combo; although, it has shipping weights is low.

Tip #2- Research, compare, and evaluate dropshipping trends

eBay is one of the places to check whether items sell online but do not use eBay to determine the price of your products as eBay's prices are relatively low.

Once you get onto eBay, one of the things you want to research is to identify the products in the different niches in the higher-priced bracket, the ones that are expensive so it can be anything like $50 or $200 or

$500 depending on the product. When you get your search results, allow it to show 'completed listings'. A completed list shows items in red or green, red being the item that did not sell and green is sold.

Look at the items only for the products you are considering to niche in. It is okay to go over this list a few times until you have about 20 products that will most likely sell out always within your niche - at least ten units per day.

From here, request for price lists from various suppliers, get shipping quotes from customs brokers as well as storage capacities for a product.

Tip #3- Utilize Amazon

Being the world's largest retailer, Amazon sells everything imaginable. Because of this, Amazon is one of the best things on the Internet to find profitable niches and other amazing possibilities that you never thought of.

Here's how you can find, using Amazon, red hot profitable niches:

First, on the main search bar's left side, you can find the 'All' tab button. Click on that button. You will see niches or a list of categories.

- Click on your chosen category and click on 'Go'.
- When the new page pops up, a list of 'sub-niches' can be seen on the left side.
- More specific sub-niches can be seen when you click on a subcategory.
- You now have specific niches! You can go down this list if you really want to.

Amazon is also a great place to help you in a specific niche as well as the product that sells the best. 'Bestsellers' can also be chosen from the navigation bar located just right under the search bar at the top of the page. You can see all the items that are currently selling the best.

Tip #4 - Put on your Marketer Cap

One of the best things you can sell with drop shipping is to sell EXPENSIVE items.

About 20% of your total sales are your average dropshipping profit. If you have a $1,000-item, you can make 20% profit which is $200 or 20% on an item that is $10 which makes you $2. If you want to start making money, start selling the big toys. Sounds simple, but in truth, you need to do more research. You also need to identify potential future competition, which are other online retailers who are selling the items you want to sell.

The roadblock here is that there is no way to find out how much money a retailer makes on each and every sale at this point unless you use a MAP procedure.

Should I choose money or passion in a niche?

It really depends on you. To some people, starting a business in dropshipping also means that they can work on a product or doing business that they love.

Whereas to some, the more cash they can receive on their bank account, the more they become motivated and they don't care what they sell.

The truth is that you want to make a profit for any kind of venture or business you are in. So, you will most likely look into a balancing act of pursuing your passion and creating a successful profit line.

Having said that, you still need to have some kind of interest into the product that you are selling because it will keep you motivated to explore even further on your audience' needs which will also help you align your content. It doesn't always mean that you will be successful when you pursue your passion.

So how do we balance the two?

Passion does lead the way. Finding profitable niches to things, items, and products that you are passionate about not only make your bank account healthy but it also makes you have fun and love what you do.

To help you discover your passion, if you have already not, let's take a look at niches that are based on your passions. Here are some questions you can ask:

- What kind of websites and blogs do you visit and interact with the most?
- What kind of accounts or pages do you enjoy and follow on social media?
- Which online stores do you usually purchase from?
- What do you think are your biggest obsessions?
- What kind of products do you usually collect or buy most frequently?
- What will you buy if you have $1000 to spend?

Next, these questions can help you in choosing a niche based on how much money you can make, then you might want to ask yourself these set of questions:

- Identify the online retailers that are currently gaining popularity and the products that they sell. (Answer these questions focusing on a few specific niche-based retailers instead of big names like Amazon)
- Which niches hold the biggest audiences?
- Which products have the highest profit margin?

- Which products are the most popular right now?

Trending Niches vs Evergreen Niches

Most retailers like an evergreen niche since it stands the test of time. Evergreen niches may include weight loss, fashion, beauty, and gaming. However, on the other hand, trending niches have instant profits and surge but it also falls in popularity pretty fast.

Tools that you can use for finding a Niche Market

To create a shortlist of niche ideas, you can use several kinds of tools so that you can identify which niche can be related to your passion or which will bring you more profit.

First, start your search with these:

- Treadhunter
- AliExpress
- Amazon

- Oberlo

Trending niches can be easily found on all of these websites. Always look out for upcoming niches and try searching for potential sub-niches that you find interesting that would complement each other.

Trending Products Blog Posts

Another thing to look out for is the updated product lists. Oberlo is one such company that regularly shares updated product lists to ensure that they are always at the forefront of today's most popular products. These lists can also help you determine what you want to niche on. Apart from that, keep an cyc out for blog posts with lists such as:

- 20 of the best gardening tools to have in 2018
- 30 Fail-proof Business ideas to make money in 2018
- Best Buy Beauty Products for Summer 2018
- Top 10 Polishes To Get your Car Shining like Brand new

Check out the products that these articles mention as well as the dropshipping products being sold and the business ideas related to it.

Wikipedia's List of Hobbies

Wikipedia's list of hobbies is a great way to find a niche of practically anything that you can think of from hobbies to passion, from crocheting to baton twirling, resin art to golfing, furniture restoration and terrariums- you will be surprised to find an extremely extensive list of outdoor and indoor hobbies. Look into the lists if your passion can be connected to those hobbies or look for niches that can be highly profitable in these categories. Some hobbies are popular enough to have a large market of followers so you can actually build an entire store dedicated to selling these products or the items that help hobbyists work on their passions.

The amazing thing about hobbies is that like-minded people didn't need to hesitate to spend some money on pursuing their hobbies or join some groups. This can help you gain an audience where you can sell your products immediately. You can build e-commerce stores on some hobbies including:

- Baking
- Various fitness niches
- Pet
- Magic
- Gardening
- Flower arranging
- Fashion
- Do it yourself
- Astrology
- Jewelry making

Google Trends

Yes, Google Trends is another tool you can use to discover your niche. What you want to look out for are niches that have a stable growth no matter how slight. Here is a list you can check out-Google Trends.

You do not necessarily need to be an expert in a niche but some experience will help you a long way. Although it is not impossible to build a brand without having some kind of experience, it may also be difficult.

Alternatively, you can make it by faking it which means that you can use Facebook ads to look for the right target audience. You can also use Instagram to engage influencers to build an audience as this can lead to sales. Having some idea about the niche you are getting into will also help you create content that resonates with your audience. No experience may render it harder to reach them and bring that traffic to your store.

On the other hand, you can also outsource these blog writing tasks to ghostwriters or someone equivalent. But most entrepreneurs do this, especially when starting out to keep costs low. As mentioned previously, it can greatly motivate you if you sell a product that you like and have some experience on that specific niche to sustain your business, especially if the money isn't hitting the profit margins like you want to.

FB Search

Another tool you can use is FB search and this tool can help you determine the amount of engagement your posts actually get. You can also see your competitors' post by using a competitor analysis tool. You can also look up at the brands that are within your niche. Search using specific keywords to search. Your search will turn up based on people, pages, photos, videos, links, and marketplace. When you look at these pages, you can see the number of followers. It will also help you understand the kind of frequency your Facebook posts need to be. You can scale quickly and have a more competitive advantage if you can post once or twice a day.

Browsing the pages that come up in your search also gives you an idea of the direction of your marketing strategy, looking through photos helps you understand the kind of material you need to create and the markets you can target.

Continue Your Research

Before you begin building your store, please be reminded of some of these things first. Before you buy ads online or spend hours promoting our website, ensure that you have already built your target audience. Here's a quick list of what to look for:

- Does your niche have fans?
- Do influencers post about this niche?
- Does your niche have events people host?
- What kinds of forums exist for people to discuss the niche?
- Are there targeting options you can use on Facebook for this niche?
- Does your niche have dedicated groups on Facebook?
- What kind of social platforms do people market your niche?

Facebook, Instagram, YouTube, and Pinterest are all popular places to look if your niches are talked about on these platforms. It is always better to put your content where it is seen, heard, and speaks because there is where your audience spends time on.

Another thing is that all of these platforms have one element in common. They are all heavy on visuals which means, stunning images and video reach out to your audience faster.

STEP 2: Looking for and Choosing your Suppliers

There are many important elements that you need to think about when choosing your dropship suppliers. In this chapter, we will explore how to find one, how to differentiate between a supplier and a retailer, and legal matters.

Finding Wholesale Suppliers

There are a number of strategies that you can use to find wholesale suppliers, some being effective and some not. There is a list of methods that you can try, starting with the most effective.

Contact the Manufacturer

Contacting the direct source is one of the best ways. Once you know the product you are planning on selling, pick up the phone and call the manufacturer who focuses on this product and asks for a list of their wholesale distributes. Contact these wholesalers and inquire about opening up an account with them. In doing so, you will be able to source a selection of products more efficiently and easily in the niche that you want.

Try Oberlo

Importing products to your online store from the suppliers can be easily done using Oberlo. You also just need to click some buttons so that you can directly ship your items to your clients. Using Oberlo, you can fulfill orders automatically, do product customization, and pricing automation.

Google It!

It may seem a pronounced solution. However, there are rules that you should follow when using Google:

- Don't judge the website by its front page. Most wholesalers' websites are outdated. While some wholesalers do put in an effort to get a good website out, don't get let down by a poorly design site.
- Use Modifiers. When searching on Google, use other kinds of keywords such as 'reseller' or 'bulk' or 'warehouse'.

Order from the Competition

This may be one way to locate a supplier - by making a small order with an opposing company. When you receive your package, use Google to find the return address to find out the original shipper. You can also contact the supplier to find out. This is not a method to rely on, but a good solution, nonetheless.

Attend Trade Shows

Attending trade shows allows you to meet and network with manufacturers and wholesalers in the niche that you want to retail in. This method works great only if you have picked your niche and the product that you want to sell within that niche. Invest a little bit of time attending these shows. Meeting your suppliers and manufacturers face to face helps build business partnerships.

Directories

A directory in supplier's database is another way of scoring a good selection of suppliers based on market or niche. Many directories use a screening process to legitimize their suppliers and ensure that they try genuine wholesalers. While these lists are beneficial, they are not something you need. Finding major suppliers can be done with a little bit of digging, especially when you've established the product or niche you won't sell. This is a nice-to-have, not a must-have. Supplier directory is a convenient method to search quickly and browse a large number of suppliers.

Before You Contact Suppliers

So now that you have a solid list of suppliers, it's time to move on to the next step - contacting them. Before you do that, get yourself equipped using these guidelines:

- You Need to Be Legal – legitimate wholesalers will need proof of your business even before you are allowed to open an account with them. Pricing is only revealed once a customer has been approved so apart from making sure your wholesale is legal, you also need to be legally incorporated so you have the right documents and licenses.

- Understand How You Appear – having a great business plan just won't cut it with wholesale suppliers as they often get these from retailers, accompanied with questions that take up their time but in the end, no order is made. Be aware that suppliers are not going to empathize with you. While they will happily help you create an account on dropshipping, don't expect them to give you discounts or even spend hours on the phone or on email with you. You need to make a purchase first because otherwise, you will earn a bad reputation which can spread quickly and hurt your relationship with other potential suppliers.

- Build credibility first before even attempting to make special requests and be definite about your business plans such as launch dates, shipping dates, and quantities and such instead of giving vague ideas. You also want to communicate your professional successes in the past because it can help with your dealings with a supplier. Your objective is to convince suppliers that dealing with you - despite your special requests - will pay off when you start to bring more business and become successful.

- A tele-conversation helps – While many are more confident about sending emails, calling them is a better prospect of securing a partnership with your supplier. Some issues just need to be tended on the phone as opposed to emails. You can send follow-up emails after a tele-conversation. Suppliers always have people calling them including people new to the business. More often than not, you'll get a sales representative that is more than happy to answer your questions.

If you are planning to call a supplier, a good tip would be to write the questions you want to ask them. It will be easier to make this call when you have your questions to ask.

Ways in Searching for Good Suppliers

In the world of dropshipping, it is important to work with the right supplier, especially since suppliers are a crucial element of this entire dropshipping process. But like everything in life, dropshipping suppliers also come in different sizes, needs, and interest.

In finding the right kind of suppliers, here are some attributes you want to look out for:

- **They have professional staff and targeted to the industry**

Suppliers who are professional also have a sales rep that is equipped with the knowledge of industry needs and they are also trained with the know-how of the industry and the product lines that they are dealing with. If you are in a niche product line, calling these sales reps and getting their invaluable insight is an asset to your dropshipping business, especially if you are not familiar with it.

- **They have Dedicated Support Representatives**

Most of the time when you contact a good quality supplier, you will usually be assigned to an individual sales representative who will not only deal with the issues you have but also ensure that they with you from the introduction, product information, and make a sale, sometimes, even after-sales. Suppliers who do not assign specific sales representatives often give you more problems because issues take longer to resolve and you usually have to end up calling and nagging them 'til the issue is resolved. Having a single supplier contact who deals exclusively with your case for solving your issues is really important and crucial.

- **They are Invested in Technology**

We did say that suppliers usually do not have updated websites. While this should not be a cause for you to reject them, quality suppliers do understand the benefits of having a well-functioning website. Most of the time, they are also easier to work with. Suppliers who provide a comprehensive product catalog online, searchable order history make your life easy too. So while wholesalers are not really tech-savvy, to begin with, engaging with one that does place importance in a good website helps in the long run.

- **They Can Take Orders via Email**

Having to make a call or manually place orders on the website is a tedious task, not only is it time- intensive, but it is also cutting back on your resources. When choosing your supplier, find one that makes ordering through email a seamless process.

- **They are Centrally Located**

A centrally-located supplier is beneficial no matter where you are. Location is imperative and a supplier that is conveniently located enable packages to be shipped and delivered within 2 to 3 business days. Suppliers located at coastal areas often take a week or more to get orders shipped and delivered. You can promote consistently your faster delivery times using conveniently located suppliers, enabling you to save more money on fees and having a happy customer.

- **They are Organized and Efficient**

Having competent staff and excellent systems is like having a well-tuned and functional website. It reduces errors, saves time, and keeps both parties happy. Incompetent staff results in botched orders and unhappy customers. The issue is that you will not know the competency of your supplier without really using it, which is why reading reviews are important.

Another way to identify good suppliers is to place small orders to get a sense of their processes, sales reps, and professionalism. This way, you can identify:

- How efficient their ordering process is
- How fast items are shipped out
- How efficient are they in following up with an invoice for tracking information
- How good is the quality of their packing

Options on Paying Suppliers

Suppliers usually accept payments in these two ways:

- **Credit Card**

Credit card payment is usually the preferred payment for suppliers, especially if you are new and establishing a presence in the industry. Credit cards are still the best options, once you have a thriving business, as they are more convenient, especially for making online payments. You also get loads of points on your card whenever you make frequent payments, too. You can also use your credit card to obtain a higher volume of purchases without dealing with the actual out-of-pocket expense.

- **Net Terms**

Net terms on an invoice are another common way to pay suppliers. When using this method, you are usually given a certain period to pay off the supplier. For example, if you have a "net 30" term, this means that you have to pay your supplier exactly 30 days from the purchase date. You can do this either by check or a bank draw. You would also need to provide credit references from the supplier before they allow your net payment terms because this means you are lending money from them.

How to Spot Fake Dropshipping Wholesalers

In a world of good suppliers, you will also come across fake and bad suppliers. Unfortunately, wholesalers who are legitimate are usually bad at marketing which makes it harder to find them. This usually means that you will find wholesalers that are not genuine. They are usually middle persons who end up in your search results before they are better marketers. You need to be more cautious if this.

You can determine if your wholesale supplier is fake or legitimate by following some of these methods:

- You are asked for monthly fees – If you are engaging a genuine wholesale, they will not impose a fee just to do business with them. If a supplier asks for a service fee or monthly membership, this is a huge red light. That said, you should also learn to differentiate between supplier directories and suppliers. Supplier directories list wholesale suppliers and they are usually efficiently organized by product types or market and go through a screening process to be sure of the legitimacy of your suppliers. A fee will be charged by these directories to keep these suppliers on their list and for website maintenance. This shouldn't be taken as a sign of the directory's illegitimacy.
- Their business is not entirely wholesale– you have to apply for a wholesale account to procure genuine wholesale pricing because this proves

that you are indeed a legitimate business. You need to be approved before you can place your first order.

While monthly fees are usually a red flag sign, there are some dropshipping fees which are legitimate. Here are some of them:

Pre-Order Fees – Plenty of dropship suppliers charge a shipping fee that ranges from $2 to $5 depending on the items that they are to ship - the size and complexity will usually determine these prizes. This is standard practice in the industry because the shipping and packing costs for individual products are higher than if they were bulk orders.

Minimum Order - You will need to place a minimum order which is usually at the lowest amount if this is your first order. This is done to filter out merchants who are only there to window shop and this also lessens time in answering questions that do not translate to meaningful businesses.

This could cause issues if you are dropshipping. If you feel that ordering a pre-order amount is too risky, you can also offer to pre-pay your supplier that applies with your shipping orders. This way, you are building credit with them and it allows you to meet the supplier's minimum requirement but also prevents you from placing a large single order without any initial orders made by your customers on your site.

STEP 3: Conduct a competitive analysis

Some of your biggest competition will come from bigger operations such as Walmart and Amazon. This doesn't mean that you should sell a product that has no competition. Produces that have no or little competition really means nobody is looking for it online or wants it. There are, of course, many other reasons a product may not have that competition. It could be poor profit margins, manufacturing issues, supplier issues, and the biggest wreck would be the difficulty in shipping the item. When starting your dropshipping business, start with products that have competition. Not only is it high in demand but it has a proven sustainable business track.

Every step you make in your drop shipping industry is being watched by your competitors. Your competitors are watching every step you make from asking reviews for your site to growing your social media following - all of this is being watched.

As time passes, they will also start monitoring the bestsellers on your site, observing the patterns based on what content you post on your social sites, and also what kind of pages you have on your store and the kind of copy you used on your sites. They want to know what you do differently. Why do you think they do this? This is competitive analysis. If you want to succeed for the long haul, the competitive analysis must be done regularly, most of all, before you begin.

How to Do a Competitive Analysis

To do a proper competitive analysis, you must first and foremost be objective and conduct thorough and in-depth research. When you conduct competitive analysis, it will help you recognize what would work for you and what doesn't work for your brand. A competitive analysis will also enable you to figure out ways that you can break out of your competition and set yourself apart. Here are some effective ways to carry out a competitive analysis:

- Know Your Competitors

When you create a competitor analysis framework, it starts with knowing who your competitors are. The competitors' lists are businesses that you consider to be your main competitor but it also includes businesses that are indirect competitions with your business. So, the first step is to identify your direct and indirect competitors. Include information about these companies such as best sellers, website, location, and anything that could help you identify which area you need to focus and what your biggest challenges are in terms of setting up your business.

- Know the Product of Your Competitors

In this section, you need to do an in-depth analysis of the services and products. An in-depth analysis includes an understanding of the competitors' products, its features, the values, and their target market for the specific product. You also need to look at how your competitors market their products and what works for them. Understanding what your customers think about the competitor's product is also crucial and how they rank and value them. All you need to find this information is by reading reviews and ratings to give you an idea.

- Know the Strengths and Weaknesses of Your Competitors

A crucial aspect of the competitor analysis is to analyze the weaknesses and strengths of your competitors. This must be done objectively when judging your competitor's services and products as if they were your own. Try to understand what it is about their product and service that makes them grow rapidly. Keep an eye out for opportunities to understand these aspects of your competitors so you can give your own product a unique selling point.

- Know the Strategies and Objectives of Your Competitors

You must always keep abreast of what your competitors are doing. It will be hard to pinpoint exactly what your competitors are planning but you can look at the various factors that are more obvious such as their marketing, their advertising, the customers they target as well as the distribution channels they use and whatever else you find about them. Observe and analyze what these methods and strategies are.

- Know the Market in Which You Function

To kickstart a thorough competitor analysis, you need to analyze competitors and also have an understanding of the market you are involved in. Not only that, but you also need to understand the potential of your own product, such as whether the demands increases or is flat for your type of product.

By doing this, it will help you understand the levels of competitions you face. If the market has sections, you may be able to find a really specific niche that interests you which you can look into branching into the future.

Understanding your surroundings and the market climate will help you shape and plan your present and future decisions.

Competitor Analysis Tips

- Search for bestseller stores that are in your niche

Some online stores may not have bestsellers list. However, you can do this hack of adding "?sort_by=best-sellers" into the URL to find them. This works for Shopify stores so you can easily find them in stores based on categories. However, some store owners have discovered this hack and have conveniently blocked these URLs so it will not work.

You can try it because there may be some stores that have not done it.

- Add items to your competitors' carts

When you add items into your competitor's carts but do not check out, you'll end up getting retargeting ads or abandoned cart emails to tell you to make your purchase complete. These emails also give you insight into how these competitors market their brand, present their products, the choice of words they use, the design, and their marketing strategy.

- Browse pages

What does your competitor have that you may want to add to your marketing arsenal? Do they have an active blog? How is your contact page presented? Do they have a list of team members on their about page? How to do they present information on their product page? Are the images used stock photos or is it taken on their own? A part of your competitor analysis needs you to analyze all these details of their store. You may not know how well these products sell and what the conversion rates are but it might be worth testing it on your store.

- Read the comments

Reading comments left on review pages, on YouTube comment sections, Facebook pages, article links, and website, or Twitter feeds will give you an idea of what the perception is from users who have used your competitor's service or product. While it can be tempting to leave a negative comment on your competitor's social media, avoid doing this. This is unethical and not something to be proud of. It will also hurt the industry that you are in.

- SEO tools

SEO tools are essential if you have an online site. You can use SEO tools to figure out specific keywords that rank high among your competitors. You will also want to create your content using these keywords so that you will be easier to find and you can drive targeted traffic to your store. Utilizing tools such as

Sport and BuzzSumo can help you identify which content gets the most social shares so that you can write more content with these keywords on to your store.

- Social media marketing

It is also good to know what kinds of social networking sites your competitors are on because that's where your audience would be too. Are they more focused on Pinterest and not Facebook and Instagram? Why is that? It is good to look into the WHY, but sometimes, having content on a site that your competitor is not will help you find a different kind of audience. You definitely do want to be on the same platforms which your competitors are on but you may also want to explore the sites that they are not and see whether these networks work for you because this could bring in a greater opportunity for your brand.

- Use Price comparison websites

Price comparison websites help you determine how your competitors price their products. While you may not always want to compete based on a price approach, it will help you position your product or service at the right price scale so that you do not end up losing too much money. With dropshipping, you will never win in the price or cost factor simply because you are not the manufacturer, only the seller. Price comparison sites such as Yahoo! Shopping, Google Shopping, BizRate, and NexTag are some of the sites to look at to determine what price to put on your product or service.

Competitor Analysis Tools

One of the tools to use in your competitive analysis is Google Alerts. This tool sends you email alerts when news about your search keyword appears. For instance, if you add your 'soap' as an alert, you will be notified when new content online appears. This can be anything from news articles, blog posts, reviews, and publications. You can also add in keywords specific to your competitors, even their brand name.

This way, you can always stay informed about what people are talking about, who's saying what and what is going on in your industry.

STEP 4- Optimize your site for e-commerce

A site optimized for e-commerce is extremely crucial in the dropshipping business model. One of the simplest platforms that you can use is Shopify as it comes with built-in, customizable apps to help you create a website, increase sales, and even market your website. It is a very easy plug-and-play option.

Of course, you can also get a web design and development company to help you create an e-commerce website, should you have a sizable budget for this.

However many newbie retailers prefer using play-and-play e-commerce, especially in the beginning. You can then explore additional website customization once you have a better idea of where your business is heading, have better funds, and add in new approaches to your site.

Why is it important to optimize your site?

Someone types out an item on Google search that is sold in your store. Unless the page of our product is properly optimized, they may not easily find your store's product. Unless you want to miss out on potential customers, you must make optimizing your site a priority.

Importance of Product Keyword Research

Each product page that you created on your site needs to be supported by research in the eyes of the buyers who search for your product. This is why, when it comes to SEO, keyword research is important. Before you optimize your page, you must know the keywords that are used to search for your type of product and what attracts the most traffic.

As a site owner for a dropshipping business, you must understand the unique and best keywords and phrases used for your products by factoring these elements:

- Relevance
- Search volume
- Ranking difficulty

You can use tools such as Google Search Console to help you identify the top queries on the net, Keywordtool.io to gain insight on consumer behavior, Unamo SEO for analyzing the competition as well as Google Keyword Planner for finding product page keywords that you can target.

- Ensure that the Name of your Product is Descriptive and Relevant

The way you name your products also affects search rankings. Utilize keywords that you identified previously to create unique yet descriptive names for your products. When naming your product, you have to ensure that they include descriptions and are on-point so that your customers will want to know about your product. The easiest way to do this is to do a Google search of the product you are selling and see what kinds of description and product names are used on the most visible pages.

- Use High-Quality Descriptions to Add Value to Your Products

Product descriptions are extremely valuable with SEO but only when it is value added. The product descriptions that your customers would want to know about include Key Features and Specification, major features, and value. You can also include model numbers, keyword variation, and brand name.

Ultimately, you also want to keep these descriptions brief yet informative but not extremely wordy. Bullet points and lists are extremely favored. Also, never copy content from the manufacturer - you want to make yours unique to your dropshipping site.

- Improve Rankings with Your Page Title

Another way to optimize your site is to include the right page titles that correspond to your product as well as improve the rates of your click-through. The title of your page should be one-of-a-kind and include the relevant keywords. Start by placing the main keyword at the front of the title but do not repeat it. Your brand name should also be included in the title for maximum effect.

- All items should have Meta Descriptions that are Unique

Rankings are not affected by keywords found in meta descriptions but you need to add them anyway as it can bring in more clicks. On top of that, you can immensely boost the rates of your click-through by formatting them with symbols and numbers and including a keyword. You should explain and give your users the information about your page. Again, do make it unique but do not make it lengthy. Shopify, the favored dropshipping site, provides a simple and intuitive editor to make changes to metadata. It also automatically generates robots.txt and sitemap.xml files to avoid problems with regards to duplicate content.

- Give your Product URLs some Attention

URLs are sometimes the least looked into optimization element. Clean and keyword friendly URLs make huge impacts on search rankings. If you have old URLs, make sure they are redirected to the new URLs on your site. Your URLs must be user-friendly and appear directly beneath the title in search engine results. Again, these URLs must be short and written in lowercase. They must include keywords as well as subfolders. Do not include any dynamic parameters and clean up elements that are unnecessary in the URL structure such as ID categories.

- Add Product Reviews

Product reviews are an ultimate must for a site. It builds trust and enables user engagement as well. When enabling product reviews for your site, make sure that the text is crawlable. You also need variety on your reviews - not all of them are going to be five-star and that's okay. The variety on feedback gives legitimacy for your products. You can get user reviews through email follow-ups, incentivizing on user interaction, at the same by time, offering discounts and raffles to those that submit feedback.

- Use images and Videos to Improve Your Chances

When creating your site, use quality product videos and images. How-to videos and 360 images of your product increase buy-in and it also compliments your keywords, headings, and product descriptions. It also boosts your sales and traffic. Quality images and videos also give credibility to your site. When including photos and videos, optimize them by using keywords in the file name and alt tags. Optimization can also be done through video and image sitemaps that ensures your product's pages are crawled quickly and effectively.

- Improve your Conversions by using a Prominent CTA

You should always have your end goal in sight when building and optimizing your site - which is to get customers to add products to their cart and complete the purchasing products by buying your products. The 'Add to Bag' option is your biggest CTA so make it stand out so that customers are focused.

- Reduce the Loading Time of Product Pages

At this day and age, flashy graphics and slow-loading pages are a big NO. User's attention span is 3 seconds and when they visit your site, they want to see the products that they are interested in without waiting for a long video to be over or pop-ups clouding their vision. Test your optimized site using the Pingdom's Performance monitoring tool to see how fast your page loads.

STEP 5- Build a customer acquisition plan

Now that you have a great product and a fantastic website, have there been any sales yet? Without customers coming to your site to purchase, you do not have any business. Announce your presence by using social media! Depending on what you are selling, use a social media account that can best show your customers what you have to offer. Facebook, Instagram, and YouTube have the highest usage to search, explore, and purchase. You can reach out to a targeted audience easily and generate sales and revenue right from the start. This will also give you the capacity to compete with the largest brands and retailers on the get-go.

Apart from this, think ahead and start optimizing your site with search engine optimization and email marketing. Allow customers who visit to opt for emailed newsletters so you can send discounts and special offer right into their inbox.

So, how do you create a customer acquisition plan? Here is where you begin.

1. Finding your users

The first step in building a customer acquisition plan is determining who your customers are. This is one of the key things to identify apart from identifying the kind of product you want to sell. There is definitely a certain demographic that you are targeting with the products and services you are offering in your dropshipping site. If you do not have a target market in mind, you are limiting your ability to effectively market your brand. Unless your brand fulfills a universal need, you are much better off narrowing your demographics to focus on a specific market, especially if you are providing a niche product. Identify your target market by age, gender, and location. These are the first elements to create a target market.

The next layer would be their interests, needs, and desires. By crafting out a profile or persona of your ideal audience, you can pinpoint a target market that best fits this persona.

2. Knowing where your Target Audience is located

Where does your persona hang out? This should be the next item to identify in your customer acquisition plan. In order to increase your chances of customer acquisition, you need to be visible at the places that they are usually on, in both offline and online spaces. Once you have this information, you can be able to develop a marketing plan to meet your target market's needs and interests. Depending on your target market's age group, they would probably frequent social media sites such as Instagram and Pinterest, and for this, you need a social media marketing plan to be visible on these sites and maintain constant contact with your target customers. Meet-up groups and communities both online and offline is another way to meet and know your target market. Target users to solve their problems. Once you have found your niche audience, do not only work to promote your products and services but also work towards sincerely engaging with them to create value and brand loyalty.

3. Incorporate Content

Developing the right content is the next step in your plan. This content must be a variety of multimedia content to promote your brand as well as facilitate customer acquisition. Your content depends on the type of product or service you are selling. Are you selling hiking gear? Having a video showcasing people using your hiking gear for their trails and hikes can provide value to your brand in a significant way. You can also alternate your content between how-to videos, lifestyle videos, photos in every angle, and culture photos. Create content that varies between entertaining and informational. Post these contents on the social media sites your target audience frequents. The more you make effort to connect, the better off your brand will be.

4. Get the Word Out

Once you have the right balance of content, you know where to post them up, and what and who your target audiences are, you need to start getting the word out on your brand. You need to get the word out not just through online avenues but also using the word-of-mouth referrals which still serves as a powerful marketing tool. Instagram and Snapchat have now become the online version of conventional word-of-mouth. People go to these sites to look at reviews, opinions, and generally what the internet says about your brand and product. You need to be on these sites to know the buzz as this also gives you the opportunity to make changes so that your word-of-mouth referrals are positive rather than negative.

5. Give Away Free Stuff

In this day and age with plenty of influencers and sponsored content, some consumers are not easily swayed by product reviews or even online word-of-mouth referrals. In order to convert these people to become your loyal customers, you need to provide them with an experience of your product and service by offering them free or discounted items. This can be done as a seasonal marketing strategy for holidays such as Christmas or New Year's, or even a buy-one-free-one for an existing customer. When giving out free items, make sure they represent what your brand or product truly is- do not give away low-quality items because this does not reflect who you are as a brand. Offer the good stuff even if it is free as it is a reflection of your brand.

6. Develop a Referral Strategy

Referrals usually serve as the core of your customer acquisition strategy especially at the beginning of your dropshipping business. You need to develop a referral strategy that encourages your users to refer other users that they feel would benefit from your product or service. For instance, you may want to offer existing users discounts or extra features when they refer a new user to your site, your product or service. The popular option is a buy-one-free-one when you enter a friend's email address or get existing users to share your social media post to a friend's wall or tag a user to specific content.

STEP 6- Analyzing Data on Your Dropshipping Store

Tracking your data usage and metrics enable you to better understand your target audience. Google Analytics can be used for your website, and Facebook, Instagram, Twitter, and YouTube all have their own analytics that you can check for data on how your customers behave for each of your posts. You will always need to test our new marketing solutions and opportunities so you have a different social media campaign for your customers.

Until and unless you do data analysis, you will know how well your site is working and how much more profitable you can make it. Analyzing and optimizing your site should be done constantly to stay current and fresh as well as make better decisions for product creation. Data analyzing isn't so much about acquiring a lot of data but also knowing what to do with it.

Examples of Data Analysis Reports

Shopify: With Shopify, you can look at your data for free on the Analytics section of your dashboard. You can find your total sales, average order value, conversion rate as well as traffic sources. Under Reports, you can look at acquisition, customers, marketing, behavior, and finances. If you sell exclusively on Shopify, you can get all of this data for free.

Google Analytics: Store owners need to subscribe and register for Google Analytics whether or not you sell exclusively on Shopify. With Google Analytics, you can tell how many users have viewed your site in real-time and what exactly are they looking at. This tool also helps you understand your customer's point of view such as the traffic to your store and what the amount of time a visitor spends on each page. You will also know the gender, age as well as bounce rate.

Tips for Analyzing Data

- **Context**

When you open and start running your store, you will want to compare its growth on a year-to-year basis to understand if your numbers are positive or negative. You can do a monthly review but most products have seasonal trends which affect these numbers on a monthly basis. Looking at data on a yearly basis will enable you to see if your traffic and sales are higher or lower according to the seasons. You may not always understand the data you are looking at. You may have a low sales day and you won't know what caused it but you can always make a hypothesis of it and test them based on the actual information.

- **Perform split AB tests**

A/B testing is extremely helpful in helping you optimize your site better. Whether it is the image you are testing or the subject line, split testing allows you to improve your store using data. You need significant data to make a change. Small changes will not be helpful to your site.

- **Pay attention to 'Top products by unit sold'**

When you look at your Shopify dashboard, it will tell you what your best sellers are. Some store owners may want to increase sales to other products to ensure that their store has an all-around sale. However, it is a good practice to focus your time and energy on what sells the best. If two to three products outperform the rest of your products, this is a good sign that you need to invest more money in advertising these products. When you do this, you need to scale fast because delaying the growth of these products will ultimately give your competitors the opportunity to catch up and you don't want that.

- **Visits by Referrer**

Look at your Shopify's analytics to see visits by Referrer as this is a good indicator of where to find your best traffic. It isn't always Facebook. By looking at where your traffic is coming from, you will find other sources of referral traffic at places that you did not initiate. This is where you can explore more and drive traffic from these channels.

- **For First Time vs Returning customers**

This depends entirely on the products you sell. If you sell hair care products, chances of you getting returning customers are high. But if you sell air or water purifiers, these are usually one-time products and your returning customers are typically low. A trick or hack to boost returning customers is to send them a VIP email within 24 hours after their purchase offering an exclusive discount to buy more products from your store.

Data Analytics Tools

Here are some excellent data analytic tools that you can use to analyze your site:

- Data Export
- Analytics Buddy
- Compass

- <u>Lucky Orange</u>
- <u>Customer.Guru</u>

Chapter 3 - Different Methods of Dropshipping Business

There are many ways that you can do dropshipping, but in this chapter, we will look at the most effective methods that you can try in 2018.

Focus your time in Marketing

Many of the aspects in dropshipping retail are automated which frees up your time in focusing solely on branding and marketing your products as well as optimizing your site. Marketing is a money maker so from the logo, website look and feel to the tone of voice, you want all these things to sync in well so that you can convert your traffic to sales. Learn to master the use of ads and optimize your website with specific keywords. These elements drive more traffic to your store and convert at least 2% of customers on a daily basis.

Your objective is to get more traffic to your site so that it can generate a good percentage of sales. SEO can help drive long-term sales simply by having you rank high on search engine results. You can do this by:

1. Creating blog content
2. Optimizing your product pages
3. Update your pages and keep it fresh
4. Use Social media to optimize being found online

Create Fantastic Offers

Sales, bundles, and offers are something EVERYONE loves! It not only makes you noticeable but also increases traffic to your site! If no products on your site are for sale, customers visiting your site will lack the motivation to purchase your products. However, the right product with the right deal will more likely make them purchase on your site.

Tie offers with celebrations or holidays or even create bundle packs. When customers love a product from your site, they will likely want to purchase more of it.

The hardest part is to get them to purchase. After that, it is pretty uphill all the way!

Avoid Underpricing Your Products

In dropshipping, the cost of products is usually close to wholesale price and it allows you to sell your products at market value and get a nice profit. Businesses, dropshipping, or otherwise is to make profits. If the cost of your product is $5, then you should be selling it for $20 so you can get profits.

As long as your prices are fair and within market value, you should be able to gain a sizeable profit from each order made on your website. Do not undercut your prices even when other retailers are doing so unless you are giving an offer or discount or a sale. Create strategies that will allow you to make more money overall.

Choose ePacket

ePacket shipping is currently the fastest and most affordable dropshipping method. It ensures quick delivery without high costs. An ePacket shipping on average would cost you under $5 for most products, so this will allow you to make a profit when you sell your product at market value. ePacket deliveries reach customers within 7 to 10 days from the date of purchase and are by far one of the best delivery methods for dropshippers to use.

Go the extra mile with customer service

As anyone going to a restaurant, if they would go back to a restaurant even if the food was mediocre but with exceptional service, chances are that the answer would be yes. People remember more of how you made them feel and the same applies to e-commerce as well. Offering great customer service is one of the best ways to stand out, especially if you are selling the same products of every merchant out there. Your customer service can be in the form of thank you cards included in the shipping packages or it could also be points that they have accumulated from multiple purchases which entitle them to a free gift! It can also be simple things like speedy response to their issues or complaints. Whatever you do, make your customers feel valued and appreciated. It is because of them that you are a success.

Stay active on your channels

You need to put in effort on a consistent and daily basis. While you do not need to spend eight hours a day working on marketing and promoting your site, you still need to commit a number of hours on a daily basis to ensure that your store is updated, relevant, and active. As your business grows, so will the number of hours you need to commit to processing orders, speak with your suppliers, ensure shipping is in route, and orders arrive promptly to your customers. You will also need to ensure that your marketing efforts are in line with your products and social media is one of the best ways to stay current and relevant, ensuring that you appear at least once a day in the minds of your customers.

Start with at least 30 items on your site

Don't make the mistake of importing hundreds of items to your site. While it can be exciting, the problem would that adding too many products too soon may be suicidal to your site. For each product you add to your site, you need to have a few quality images, product descriptions, and keywords. Doing all of this in a short span of time can be time-consuming and exhausting, especially if you are still stuck in your day job. Adding the product incrementally, starting with 30, would be best as you can write quality descriptions and maintain focus to start your sales and understand how your audience reacts on your site. You need to get one great product to land a sale and not 100 products. Stay focused and start small, building your way up.

Monitor your competition

As always, you need to keep your friends close and your enemies closer. Monitor your competition's social media and their websites regularly. Like their page and you'll also receive updates on their products and the promotions they have. By paying attention to what they do, you'll also have a better idea on how to sell your products on your store. Do not rip-off content but use it as inspiration to understand what makes or breaks attention. This not only helps bring in the audience to your site but it also helps you do better in marketing your own products.

Chapter 4 - Common Dropshipping Mistakes to Avoid

By now, it does seem like dropshipping is a pretty straightforward retail business and any person would jump at the opportunity to make a business with dropshipping. The advantages are immense and one of the biggest pull factors is the costs involved to set a dropshipping business, which is next to nothing.

Despite the pretty straightforward plan, you will need to understand and know what your responsibilities are as well as the mistakes that you might end up getting into. In this chapter, we will look into common mistakes retailers often make in dropshipping so you can avoid them.

Worrying About Shipping Costs

Although shipping costs can be a pain, this isn't productive to worry. Your priorities need to be strategically aligned to increase sales and depending on where your orders come from, your shipping costs will be in a different range. So in the spirit of increasing your profits, a good thing to start with is setting a flat shipping rate. It is straightforward and easy for your customers and it will be easier for you.

Relying Too Much on Vendors

Putting your trust in your vendor can be a forum for plenty of problems ahead. Having one vendor, for example, can mean that they may raise prices for you or if they go out of business or the items run out can also make you go out of business. What would you do then?

Having a backup supplier is what you should do. When doing business in dropshipping, it is always good to write a contract with your vendors to ensure that both of you know each other's end of the bargain.

Expecting Easy Money

As we already know, dropshipping does provide a good level of convenience that does make your job a simpler one. Despite that, you need to be aware of the competition ahead of you and how important it is to market your product. This needs research as well as a unique approach that makes your product stand out amongst the masses. Don't expect money to roll in without putting in the work needed and time to see your product and your site lift out.

Making Order Information Difficult to Access

Make things easy and clear for your customers also means providing the estimated shipping dates so your customers know what to expect. Keeping your customers informed of the product they are buying, the way they make payments, the information they are keying into your site as well as how long they will need to wait until their items arrived are all the things you need to put in black and white. Not only will this help you troubleshoot problems, but your customers will be happy with the information they can access.

Not Enough Brand Display

The one major drawback of dropshipping is that it can be hard to ensure that your brand is prominent to your customers, not only in the look and feel, but also the entire customer experience. You don't want your customers to forget you. You need to work extra hard to insert your brand as much as possible in every corner you can. One of the best things you can do is to ensure you develop a good working relationship with your supplier and get them to insert custom packaging for you to remind them of you and show them you care about their experience at the same time.

Botching Order Changes and Cancellations

Your online customers change their minds faster than the ones who shop at regular stores. This is bound to happen, and for this, you need a backup plan as well. You want to ensure that your customer is efficiently and accurately refunded. Some vendors will immediately go ahead and make the order and you'll end up with a negative review on your site. To avoid this, speak to your vendor first before confirming things with your customer. While your customers wait for confirmation, let them know you have received their request and are working on making the necessary refunds or changes.

Mishandling Damaged or Lost Items — plus Other Shipping Issues

The minute a customer experiences problems with their order; their frustrations are immediately directed at you. When this happens, you need to be prepared to offer your customers an easy and quick solution. Be sure that you create a process for managing and handling problematic orders, so you can keep your customers happy.

Return Complications

Setting up a system for returns will be beneficial not only for your sanity but also to lessen the time your customers need to wait for a result. Organized and systematic approaches to problems not only keep your customers happy but it also shows you are professional.

Chapter 5 - Tips and Tricks in Dropshipping

Tips and tricks are always great for anything new that you are learning. It makes us do things better, more efficiently, in less time and achieve better results. Here are some tips to master your online dropshipping business

Keep your eye on the ball

Your main goal is to create profits, right? So that should be your focus. Do not get carried away by flashy graphics and so call 'must-haves' for your website or even long content that apparently 'speaks' to your audience. You do not want to lengthen the time it takes for your customers to decide to purchase your product. The idea is to get them to your site, browse for what they want, click on the product, read a short description, and click on Add to Cart > Proceed to Checkout. Keep things moving forward and avoid anything that detracts from this mission.

Think like a customer

One of the reasons why you need to stick to a niche that you know and one that you are passionate about is so you understand customer pain points. What do you look for when you are on someone's website? What do you expect to find there? What kind of buying process makes you feel that you purchase things fast? What makes you like the website you usually purchase from? Knowing the pain points yourself makes you understand what your customers want and how your product can help them accomplish their needs.

SEO your site

Part of your marketing should also be SEO. SEO is not dead so long as keywords are still used to search for anything and everything on the internet. You need to use SEO wisely not only on your website but also on your social media which is from content, titles, tags, image tags, and descriptions - the whole nine yards. You will be found much easier through specific keywords.

Product Reviews

The best way for any customer to know that the products that they are purchasing are value for money is by reading reviews. Customers will click on products that have higher ratings and the likelihood of them purchasing it is if has good reviews and high ratings. DO not cheat on your reviews. If you have a product that always gets bad reviews - trash it. When you do, let your customers know that you are discontinuing it because this will help increase their confidence in your site. The fact that you have heard them, and you are doing something about it increases brand trust.

Mix your marketing

There are many ways to reach your customers depending on who they are and what they do. For most dropshipping marketing methods, social media marketing and email marketing is the way to go. But you should not rely on it entirely. On and off, it is also good to meet with your customers and see who they are. Give product giveaways, hold online workshops or seminars, have an online meet-and-greet, feature your customers using your product, or give them a shout out!

Make your logistics work well

Have strong and clear agreements on any potential logistical issues that you may encounter in your dropshipping business. Outline these in your contract and also have this on your website. Inform customers what to do if they have returned. Outline this with your supplier as well and establish standard operating procedures for returns, damaged items, and so on. Outline what the shipping costs are as well between yourself and the supplier and what is the expected delivery date for your items between supplier and customer.

Establish your relationship with your supplier

Establishing and maintaining close relationships with your suppliers ensure that you can also extend the benefits to your customers. When your supplier trusts you, there will be many things that you can get done such as offer personalized packaging to your customers, ensuring speedy shipping, or have lesser time in managing any issues you have to deal with if there are any delays. Collaboration is based on trust, and the soonest you establish trust, the better.

Communicate your Product Strategy

Strong product descriptions ensure higher success rates of purchasing. This information is critical to your customer. They want to know what they are buying and the better you describe your product, the faster it would be for your customers to make a purchasing decision. Do not give long and vague descriptions and also do not put on duplicate content. Duplicate content will be penalized by search engines.

Chapter 6 - Making $100,000 A Year in Dropshipping Revenue

If you are looking for a fast way to make $100,000, this chapter will not solve that problem. However, this chapter will help you gain the necessary information and tips needed to ensure that you not only make that $100,000 in your first year but also repeat this over and over again for each year you are in business.

<u>Scaling Your Business</u>

In order to reach your goal of $100,000 in revenue in your dropshipping business, one needs to know when the time is to scale your business. Only by doing so can you be able to generate larger revenue that meets your business goals at the end of the day. The best way to grow your dropshipping business is to back look into the ads that are performing well.

Redirect a portion of your profits into those ads to capitalize on the ads performance to your intended customer pool. Reinvesting the profits back into your business will ensure that you keep your money rolling within it in order to make it more successful in the long run. In the start, it is usually the norm that business owners do not take a salary (maybe in the first year or two). They keep channeling their profits into the business to grow it further until it becomes more sustainable and competitive.

Upselling

Another approach successful dropshippers make is to make a sale of the same product to an existing customer. This strategy works as it's easier to sell something to an existing customer than to a new one. For instance, if you have sold essential oils of a particular flavor to a customer before, you stand a good chance of having a repeat order for essential oils of a different flavor. As consumers, if we already have a liking to certain things, the chances of us buying those products again are high and this is a strategy that dropshippers have used from time to time. Offering free gifts and discounts for multiple or bulk purchases to customers can be used as another selling strategy to increase revenue for your business.

Leveraging On Apps

For the novice drop shipper, there are many tools at your disposal to enable you with content and marketing tactics for your business. Some of these apps are:

- Shopify - An e-commerce platform that allows one to set up an online store to market your products
- Buzzsumo - A research and monitoring tool that finds ideas that are trending on social media platforms
- Lucky Orange - A tool that is designed to optimize and convert customer feedback in order to make your website perform better
- UserTesting - A tool in which a third party can visit your online store and provide feedback into areas in which you can improve on your website

These are just some of the apps that can be found online for you to test out and experiment with. Whichever app that you choose, you will be able to get an app that can help you overcome any issues that you may have with your online business platform.

Growing Your Business Using Data

In any business, be it the traditional or online method, data is vital in growing the business in order to stay relevant and to stay ahead of the competition. Using Google Analytics and Facebook conversion pixel data, you will be able to track every single data to grow your business. You will be able to know specific details of your customer, for example, their locality and the path they took to your website which generated the sale in the end. This will, in turn, allow you to determine what works and what doesn't work on your website to enable a farther reach to a larger pool of customers.

Must-Do to Achieve Your $100,000 Goal

None of the above can ever take place if you do not do or complete these items stated below which are identifying your niche, working with a supplier you trust and have good relationships, getting to know your competitors, and getting the word out.

Identifying a Target/Niche Market

This one is no brainer - to determine a product/service that is required by your local clientele but can't be found or provided by any existing local vendor. Should you be able to provide such a product at reasonable prices and good product quality, your business will be more attractive to your potential clientele.

It is also equally important that, when you are in this phase, is not only to look for a product/service but something that also generates a healthy profit at the end of the sale. This is because a large part of your business at the start will be on marketing and ad campaigns to attract potential customers. Hence, selecting a product/service that is in a niche and provide an attractive profit margin is vital for the sustainability of your business.

Also, you may want to consider shipping costs when identifying a product/service for your dropship business. Since most dropshippers get their supplies from overseas vendors, if the cost of shipping is high for that particular product, it will push the selling price higher and may deter customers from purchasing it at the end. So, you will need to look at something that is not too expensive to be shipped which will also allow you to provide "free shipping" options to your customer in order to generate a higher growth of sales.

Understanding Your Competition

Once you have a pretty good idea of what you would be selling, the next step is to scope out your competition and see what they are doing. What are they selling? How much are they offering for their products? What sort of marketing that they are using to reach out to potential consumers. What differentiation are they using to set them apart from the rest? Doing constant research will not only enable you to differentiate yourself from the competition but in the long run, it will also allow your business to evolve with the market trends and ever-changing competition.

One important thing to remember in this business is not only will you be competing against other dropshippers, but also against bigger companies such as Amazon, ebay, and AliExpress to name a few. And one of the more prominent mistakes novice dropshippers make at the start is working on/with a product/service that has little or no competition. This is one tell-tale sign that there is no demand in the market for this specific product/service. This could be due to numerous factors such as low-profit margins and product quality issues as examples. Hence, it is always important to acquire a product/service that has competition because that ultimately shows that there is a demand and will be a profitable business venture in the long run.

Getting the Word Out

The next step in this venture is to set-up a platform/website that will allow you to list down your products/services to your targeted clientele. A simple e-commerce platform such as Shopify, Squarespace, or Weebly would allow anyone with limited knowledge in website design to get a dropshipping business up and running in order to get that highly sort after first sales.

For those that are starting off using a website to market their products/services, it is always advisable to use the plug-and-play options offered by these e-commerce platforms until a sustainable revenue starts coming in, then you can explore your options of hiring a web design team to make additional customizations on your website.

On that note, just opening and running a website isn't a sure-fire way of reaching out to your target market. One must proactively market their business on social media using platforms such as Twitter, Instagram, and Facebook to reach out to potential clientele.

Constant engagements via tweets, posts, and videos will generate the right kind of buzz to attract business in order to start generating revenue for your site.

Working with a Supplier

Another key to any successful business is having a good partnership with your suppliers/vendors. This also holds true for the dropshipping business as most of your suppliers will originate from another country. Are they quick in their responses and do you both understand each other well in your daily communications? If you are not truly confident enough on this, then it is very important to look around for other potential suppliers to work with. Having a good supplier will be the make-or-break factor for your business in the long run.

One easiest and quickest way to know how to navigate in choosing a right supplier is to learn from the experiences of other dropshippers in the past. Here, you can look up business and tech blogs about dropshipping and learn from the experience of others in order not to make the same costly mistakes.

Conclusion

If you ever dreamt of running your own business with an easy and simple retail model, dropshipping is for you and where you start. Don't worry about failing. Dropshipping involved very minimal startup costs, and honestly, there is no failure unless you do not put in the necessary time and effort it takes to get the business off the ground.

Most often than not, many dropship retailers go into the business without any clue except to succeed in the e-commerce world. By reading this guide, you are more equipped than any of the new entrepreneurs because you have made this step, so do your research, learn, and find out what the fundamentals of dropshipping. You are already 80% equipped and ready to go!

Go out there and create a business with value and you will be on your way to a successful business. Don't think about making money fast but have the desire to create value and change the lives of the people that purchase your product.

Description

If you are planning on becoming an e-commerce entrepreneur, specifically in the art of dropshipping, then this book is for you, as you will see many benefits. The beauty of dropshipping is that you don't need to keep actual stock or inventory of the items you want to sell. In this book, we will look at all the beginner information you would need to kick start your first every dropshipping business.

You will be filled in with the details on how to start a dropshipping store, and most importantly, how to keep it. Dropshipping is among the easiest and profitable businesses in the e-commerce world, especially for those without a huge capital to work and run with, but they are still interested to sell and make money.

This book gives a comprehensive guide on what dropshipping is, a good introduction as well as who is it for, who it isn't for, and the pros and cons. You will also learn how to select a niche, the various methods involved in dropshipping as well as risks or common mistakes in dropshipping.

You will also be guided on finding the right suppliers in your business because suppliers are the backbone of any dropshipping site.